GUIDED READING

Editor: Carla Hamaguchi
Illustrator: Linda Weller
Cover Illustrator: Rick Grayson
Designer/Production: Moonhee Pak/Carrie Carter
Cover Designer: Barbara Peterson
Art Director: Tom Cochrane
Project Director: Carolea Williams

Table of Contents

Introduction · 3

Building a Balanced Literacy Program · · · · · · · · · · · · · · · · **4**
Reading Components · 5
Writing Components · 7
Reading Strategies · 8
Focus Skills · 12

Guided Reading · **13**
A Guided Reading Lesson Format · · · · · · · · · · · · · · · · · · 14
Sample Lessons
      Buttons Buttons (Emergent Level) · · · · · · · · · · · · · · 16
      Lunch with Cat and Dog (Fluent Level) · · · · · · · · · · 18
      Long Ago and Today (Nonfiction, Emergent Level) · · · · 20
      How & Why Animals Hide (Nonfiction, Fluent Level) · · · 22
Before Guided Reading
      Discussion and Questions · · · · · · · · · · · · · · · · · · 26
      Activities · 27
During Guided Reading
      Discussion and Questions · · · · · · · · · · · · · · · · · · 30
      Activities 31
After Guided Reading
      Discussion and Questions · · · · · · · · · · · · · · · · · · 32
      Activities 33

Writing Activities · **39**

Using Leveled Books for Other Reading Formats · · · · · · · **43**
Independent Reading · 43
Shared Reading · 44
Home Reading · 45

Assessment · **48**
Running Records · 48
Other Assessment Methods · 52
      Anecdotal Records
      Retelling
      Reading Inventories
      Checklists

List of Leveled Books
Fiction · 58
Nonfiction · 61

Introduction

Guided Reading provides a wealth of ideas and activities for using leveled books for guided reading and other activities in a balanced literacy program. This book provides an explanation of what guided reading is and presents a lesson format that can be used with any leveled book. Specific lesson plans in the book provide you with a better understanding of the process. You will find activity ideas to do with your students before, during, and after guided reading and follow-up activities to extend students' interactions with the books.

Although leveled books are primarily used for guided reading, they can be used for other reading formats. The Using Leveled Books for Other Reading Formats section (pages 43–47) explains some ways to use leveled books for other reading formats, such as shared reading and independent reading.

The Assessment section (pages 48–57) provides various ways to assess students' reading levels and behaviors. Running records is a common method used with guided reading. A brief explanation and sample running record form provide an overview of this method of assessment. Anecdotal records, reading inventories, and checklists are other ways to monitor students' reading abilities. Copy the reproducibles (pages 51 and 53–57), and use them to assess your students.

At the end of the book, you will find lists of over 200 fiction and nonfiction leveled student books offered by Creative Teaching Press. These books have been carefully developed to provide readers with text they can successfully read on their own. Each book is leveled from A–Q (A being the easiest). Each list is ordered by book level and includes a brief description of the subject matter that each book covers. Approximate grade levels for each book are also provided as a guideline.

The activities and innovative ideas are great for new teachers and experienced teachers who are already doing guided reading groups but want to enhance student learning. With all this information at your fingertips, you are now ready to conduct guided reading groups with your students!

Building a Balanced Literacy Program

The development of skills and strategies is an ongoing part of a balanced literacy program and occurs within the context of the reading and writing students are doing in the classroom. Skills can be taught formally when students experience specific difficulties or when you anticipate difficulty with a particular text. Skills are tools that learners use to make sense of a story when they read and to communicate effectively when they write. Most importantly, skills become strategies when learners apply them to solve their reading and writing difficulties. Developing strategies should be the focus of all skill instruction. See pages 8–10 for reading strategies and page 12 for a list of focus skills.

The components of a balanced literacy program include

Reading
- modeled reading (read aloud)
- shared reading
- guided reading
- independent reading

Writing
- writing aloud
- shared writing
- guided writing
- independent writing

Reading Components

It is important to engage children in a variety of reading formats so they will gain the support and background they need in order to become proficient readers.

Modeled Reading—Read Aloud

Reading aloud is an important part of a balanced literacy program. Read to students several times a day in the classroom, and encourage parents to spend at least 15 minutes a day reading to their children at home. Reading aloud makes a significant impact on the developing reading skills of young children. It builds comprehension, vocabulary, and listening skills, and it exposes students to good literature written on a level higher than their instructional level.

Enrich your program by choosing read-aloud titles that extend student learning. Students will gain information and knowledge they can access when working on their own. For example, by reading *From Seed to Plant* by Gail Gibbons, you introduce background knowledge and vocabulary relating to the life cycle of plants. This extends learning in *The Seed Song* from the *Learn to Read* series. Or, by reading aloud several versions of *City Mouse and Country Mouse,* you acquaint students with the story, supply background knowledge, and introduce important vocabulary. This introduction will help a student independently read the version of the book matched to his or her instructional level.

Shared Reading

Shared reading is a powerful tool for teaching students what reading is all about. Students at all developmental levels are invited to join in the reading of a Big Book, poem, chant, or pocket chart story. The enlarged print in shared reading materials encourages the whole group to participate. Modeling and student participation occur simultaneously. The emphasis during these sessions is on the joy and satisfaction of reading.

Lead students to make predictions about the story, identify familiar words and phrases, recognize new words and phrases, and read character names. Introduce text by pointing out features such as title, author, illustrator, and illustration style. Have students make predictions about the text by answering open-ended questions such as *What do you think this book will be about? Where will it take place? Who are the characters*? Depending on the skills emphasized, you may discuss the title page, the page count, and features of print such as indented lines, capital letters, and punctuation. Students enjoy reading Big Books again and again during shared reading, and those books become favorite choices during independent reading.

Guided Reading

Guided reading is a small-group instructional model that allows the teacher to select appropriate text for a small group of students (who are similar in strengths and needs) to provide instruction that targets specific reading strategies. The purpose of guided reading is to encourage independent reading. The focus is on mastery of reading strategies and elements of literature.

During guided reading, work with small groups of students who each have a copy of the same book. A guided reading session is a good time to model and reinforce emergent-level strategies such as one-to-one correspondence, return sweep, locating known and unknown words, letter/sound correspondence (phonics), context clues, and visual searching.

As students develop fluency, give them a book they have not read before that matches their instructional level. Have each student work through the text while getting support from you and other readers. Discuss with students the strategies that help them comprehend the reading selection. This is where the real work of reading occurs. After several successful readings of the book, students can take the book home to read to their parents.

Independent Reading

Students need many opportunities to read independently. Create a print-rich, reader-friendly classroom by making the following materials accessible:

- Big Books from previous shared reading sessions
- little books mastered during guided reading
- student-created books modeled after shared Big Books
- previously introduced pocket chart sets
- wall stories, story murals, and poetry charts
- trade books with text suitable for readers of different levels
- a listening post with appropriate trade books

Writing Components

Reading and writing are inseparable in a balanced literacy program. They are mutually supportive processes—growing expertise in one area influences the other. Encourage students to write through writing aloud and shared, guided, and independent writing sessions.

Writing Aloud

Write on a chalkboard or chart in front of students, and "think aloud" about the text as you write. This provides a powerful model on how to write and exposes students to writing conventions such as spacing, punctuation, capitals, and spelling. Many teachers write the morning message (a brief description of what is happening in the classroom or other noteworthy events) "aloud."

Shared Writing

During a shared writing session, students write with you—it is a collaborative effort. As you guide the process, students supply ideas and input. Invite students at all developmental levels to participate. Shared writing offers an ideal way for students to write original stories, thank-you letters, invitations, poems, class news, and information books or to write about shared experiences such as guest speakers or field trips. Use shared writing to create innovations and retellings of books students enjoyed during shared reading.

Guided Writing

During a guided writing session, the student does the writing while receiving support and guidance from you and other students. On the emergent level, the guided writing session may be fairly structured. For example, group members could repeat and write the same sentence of a writing frame. You may comment on what the writers are doing correctly and supply missing elements to complete the sentence.

Independent Writing

A language-rich environment is not complete without many opportunities for students to write on their own. Encourage writing with journals, reading response logs, dramatic play centers with writing supplies, classroom mailboxes, student writing boxes, and observation journals in the science center. The simple text and patterned language in leveled books provide a secure and inviting framework for students' written responses. After they read the books, some students will spontaneously adopt the language pattern and write their own versions.

Reading Strategies

Learning to read is a complex process that requires more than just looking at letters on a page. It requires a person to recognize written symbols (letters of the alphabet), associate sounds to symbols, blend sounds to form distinct units (words), organize the units into strands (sentences), and translate the strands into a coherent and meaningful message. To read successfully, a student must master the following skills:

Visual Scanning
Recognize individual letters, letter order, and whole words.

Sounding Out
Match distinct sounds to written symbols and combine those sounds and symbols together to form words.

Analyzing Sentence Structure
Use rules of grammar, mechanics, and spelling to connect words to form sentences.

Deriving Meaning from Text
Rely on prior knowledge and real-life experiences to see and understand the written message.

Learning to read is not an automatic process—it must be taught. Students need practice looking at, listening to, and deriving meaning from words. They need to understand how a message they say aloud can be communicated through symbols on paper.

Successful readers use a variety of techniques or reading strategies to help them scan text, sound out letters, analyze sentence structure, and "translate" the sentences into a meaningful message. These strategies can be grouped into three distinct categories, or cueing systems—semantic, syntactic, and graphophonic.

Semantic Strategies
Students "read for meaning" and identify unfamiliar words by
- using clues in the pictures and in the context of the story (picture clues, context clues)
- comparing what they are reading to what they already know (prior knowledge)

Syntactic Strategies

Students study sentence structure and identify unfamiliar words by

- looking at verb tense and subject–verb agreement (grammar)
- attending to predictable language patterns in written text (grammar)

Graphophonic Strategies

Students associate spoken sounds with printed letters. They identify unfamiliar words by

- sounding out individual letters and letter combinations (letter sounds)
- looking at letter sequence and "chunks" of the word (letter patterns)

Semantic, syntactic, and graphophonic strategies are interdependent. When a student reads, he or she usually relies on more than one cueing system at a time. Consider the following sentence:

I can <u>read</u> a book.

If a student is unfamiliar with the underlined word, he or she can use semantic strategies (context clues, prior knowledge) to identify the word as *read.* However, one can also *make* a book, *drop* a book, *cover* a book, and so on. By using graphophonic strategies to sound out the letter *r*, the student has a better chance of identifying the word correctly.

But what about the following example:

Yesterday, I <u>read</u> a book.

Semantic and graphophonic strategies are not enough. The student also needs syntactic cues to identify the word as past tense and to pronounce it correctly—*/red/* instead of */reed/*.

Beginning readers must be able to use all three cueing systems in a coordinated way. By cross-checking cues as they read, students confirm their understanding and gain competence in all three areas.

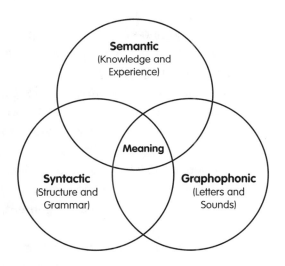

Reading Strategies Reminder

The first step in becoming a strategic reader is figuring out ways to decode and define new words. In order for students to comprehend what they read, they must first have the ability to decode unfamiliar words and determine their meaning. Students must monitor their reading to make sure that the words make sense, sound right, and look right. The key is for students to have a variety of strategies at their fingertips that they can internalize and use independently when they encounter new or difficult words.

In advance, make a class set of the Reading Strategies Bookmark (page 11), and copy each strategy from the bookmark onto a piece of chart paper. Cut out the bookmarks. Give each student a bookmark to decorate. Then, use the information at the bottom of this page to introduce each strategy. Explain how a strategy is used during reading. Provide examples to help students understand each strategy. Invite them to use their bookmark during guided reading or their independent reading.

<u>Reread the sentence.</u>
Remind students to reread the sentence more than once and think about what word might make sense.
<u>Sound out the word.</u>
Show students how to blend the sounds of the word together and try to pronounce it.
<u>Use picture clues.</u>
Encourage students to review the pictures on the page and see if the pictures provide any clues to help them figure out the unfamiliar word.
<u>Look for "chunks" in the word.</u>
Have students look for letter chunks (parts) in the word that might be familiar. Invite them to read each chunk separately and then blend the chunks together to sound out the entire word (e.g., unknown word: *fantastic*; chunks: *fan-tas-tic*).
<u>Connect to a word you know.</u>
Tell students to think of a word that looks like the unknown word. Have them compare the two words and use the known word to figure out the meaning of the unfamiliar word (e.g., unknown word: *judgement*; known word: *judge*).
<u>Read on for clues.</u>
Tell students that when they reach an unfamiliar word, they should read on a bit and try to think about what might make sense. Then, have them go back and reread the sentence with the word they think makes the most sense.

Reading Strategies Bookmark

Reread the sentence.

Sound out the word.

Use picture clues.

Look for "chunks"
in the word.

Connect to a word
you know.

Read on for clues.

Reread the sentence.

Sound out the word.

Use picture clues.

Look for "chunks"
in the word.

Connect to a word
you know.

Read on for clues.

Focus Skills

The following is a list of skills to introduce and teach during guided reading sessions.

Emergent Readers
Locating the front and back of the book
Locating the title and title page
Locating the top and bottom of the page
Locating where to begin reading on a page
Understanding left-to-right progression and return sweep (directionality)
Grasping the concept that print conveys meaning
Identifying word spacing
Finding the first and last word in a sentence
Having one-to-one correspondence
Recognizing letters
Understanding basic punctuation (period, question mark)
Reading high-frequency words

Early Readers
Building prior knowledge
Developing knowledge of concepts of word space, first/last word, one-to-one correspondence
Beginning to use reading strategies
Taking risks without fear of making errors
Using pictures as means of cross-checking
Using first and last consonant to sound out word
Retelling the story
Correctly using punctuation marks
Correctly using lowercase and capital letters
Reading for meaning
Self-correcting
Integrating strategies by using one strategy to cross-check another
Inferring more from the text to fully comprehend the author's intent

Fluent Readers
Increasing fluency
Increasing ability to read text independently
Integrating reading strategies
Understanding basic literary elements

Guided Reading

There are several positive benefits from guided reading.

- It helps deepen understanding of the text.
- It presents many opportunities for specific teaching in context as necessary.
- It encourages silent reading.
- It allows the teacher to more accurately address students' needs by grouping students of similar ability together.

Preparing for Guided Reading

- Determine each student's reading level by completing a running record (see pages 48–50).
- Select text at the student's instructional level (90–94% accuracy).
- Organize students into groups of four to six based on their current reading level. Groups can also be organized by students' need to learn a specific reading skill or strategy. For example, you may meet with a group of students who all need practice with the reading strategy of using a picture clue.
- Choose appropriate text and format for each reading level, and choose current strategy use for each group of students.
- Give each student a copy of the same text. Have groups work with you or with each other to read text at their instructional level. When students are reading at 95–100% accuracy rate, they are at mastery level. Students who read below 90% accuracy rate are at frustration level.

Tasks to Complete During Guided Reading

- Assess the developmental level of the students.
- Identify the focus reading strategies and appropriate skill work for each group.
- Constantly monitor and evaluate the students' progress using both formal (reading records) and informal (observational checklists) methods.

A Guided Reading Lesson Format

The following pages describe a sample format to use for each guided reading lesson. Choose an appropriate book for your reading group, and follow the five steps. Remember that this is just a guideline; you may need to modify these steps to meet the needs of your students. The sample lessons on pages 16–23 contain examples of how to use the same guided reading lesson format with different leveled books. Use the template on pages 24 and 25 to write your own guided reading lesson plans.

❶ Story Introduction

- Read the title and the author and illustrator's names.
- Talk about the cover illustrations.

❷ Story/Picture Walk

- Assess students' prior knowledge.
- Cover text if desired, and have students predict the story line through the pictures.
- Highlight and clarify new vocabulary and concepts.
- Explain unusual language or language patterns.
- Model and call attention to appropriate reading strategies.

❸ First Reading

The teacher models reading. (The teacher has the only copy of the book.)
- Model the language patterns and concepts about print.
- Model the awareness and use of reading strategies.

Students read silently, or the teacher reads aloud as students follow along. (Each student has a copy of the book.)
- Ask focus questions.
- Guide students to silently read a selection.
- Discuss the meaning of text, and invite students to read aloud to confirm their answers.

4 **Second Reading** (Each student has a copy of the book.)

- Choose one of the following options:
    1. Have students read aloud simultaneously.
    2. Have students read quietly but simultaneously.
    3. Ask students to read silently.
- Prompt and praise students' reading strategy use and awareness of concepts of print.
- Discuss the story.
    1. Talk about the literary elements.
    2. Talk about ideas and feelings about the story to connect it to students' lives.
    3. Retell the story.
- Present the skill lesson.
    1. Talk about concepts of print, vocabulary, and language structure.
    2. Highlight sight words.
    3. Discuss literary elements.

5 **Independent Practice or Follow-up Activities**

- Have students read independently or in pairs.
- Invite students to choral read.
- Ask students to respond in writing.
- Have students participate in one or more follow-up activities. (See pages 33–35 for activity ideas.)

Buttons Buttons
SAMPLE LESSON—EMERGENT LEVEL

Purpose
- Learn concepts of print such as directionality and one-to-one correspondence, use picture clues to figure out unfamiliar words, and locate parts of a book (e.g., cover, title page)
- Identify describing words

Key Concepts
- size
- shape

Vocabulary
round, square, lost, belly

Story Introduction and Story/Picture Walk

- Show the book cover. Ask *What do you think this book will be about? How many buttons do you see? What color are the buttons? What shapes are the buttons?*
- Point to the title of the book. Say *This is the title.* Ask *How many words are in the title? What letter do you see at the beginning of each word? What do you think the title of this book is?*
- Read the title of the book, the author's name, and the photographer's name. Tell students that the photographer is the person who took the pictures. Explain how these pictures are photographs versus illustrations.
- Show the title page. Say *This is the title page.*
- Show page 2. Point to the left side of the page and ask *How many buttons are there?* Point to the right side of the page and ask *How many buttons are there?*
- Show page 3. Ask *What colors are the buttons on this page?*
- Show page 4. Ask *What size buttons do you see?* (Point out the little buttons and the big buttons.)
- Show page 5. Ask *What animals do you see?*
- Show page 6. Ask *What shapes are the buttons?*
- Show page 7. Ask *What has happened to the little boy's buttons? What happened after he lost them?*
- Show page 8. Ask *What buttons do you see on the two children?*

First Reading

- Say *Let's read our book and look at many different kinds of buttons.*
- Read the book to students. Point to the words as you read them. Say the name of the first letter of each

One button.   Two buttons.   Red buttons.   Blue buttons.

Little buttons.   Bear buttons.   Big buttons.   Pig buttons.

word that describes the button. Say its name and sound. Pause so students can use picture clues to figure out the unfamiliar words. Ask *Can you think of a word that starts with that sound?* Say the sound again.

Square buttons. Round buttons. Lost buttons. Found buttons.

Second Reading

- Give each student a copy of the book.
- Ask students to point to the title on the cover of the book. Say *Let's read the title, the author's name, and the photographer's name.*
- Have students read the story aloud. Ask students to point to the words as they read them.
- Monitor students' reading behavior.

Belly buttons!

Discussion

- Ask students how many buttons they are wearing. Ask them what colors, shapes, and sizes their buttons are.

Mini–Language Lessons

- Say *We're going to find words that tell us how buttons look. They are called describing words.*
- Ask students to turn to page 3. Ask them what colors the buttons are. Ask them to put their finger under each word as you read it.
- Continue in this manner with the remaining pages.

Follow-up Activities

- Have students draw a picture of the buttons they are wearing that day. Tell them that their picture needs to show the size, shape, and color of their buttons.
- Make a class graph that shows the number of buttons each student is wearing.
- Have students work in groups of four to sort a pile of buttons according to color, size, and shape.

Lunch with Cat and Dog

SAMPLE LESSON—FLUENT LEVEL

Purpose
- Use the following reading strategies: visual screening, sounding out, analyzing sentence structure, and deriving meaning from text

Key Concepts
- fractions
- math language

Vocabulary
most, big, little, equal to

Story Introduction

- Give each student a book. Take a few minutes to activate the prior knowledge students have about sharing. Invite them to tell about a time when they shared food with a friend or a sibling.
- Discuss math concepts such as most, big, little, equal to, and numbers. Remind students that pictures can also represent numbers.
- Ask students to look at the cover. Give them a set amount of time—approximately 15 seconds. Ask students to tell you what they see in the picture on the cover.
- Write student responses on index cards to create word cards. Words might include *lunch*, *watermelon*, and/or *menu*.
- Ask students what they think the story will be about. Remind them to read the title and look at the pictures to make their prediction.
- Ask students what type of story they think this is—fiction or nonfiction. Define both terms, if necessary. Discuss with students clues that might lead them to the correct answer.

Story/Picture Walk

- Preview the book with students by having them browse through the pages. Ask them to pay special attention to the pictures. Explain the purpose for browsing. Tell students they are browsing to help find clues as to whether Cat and Dog know how to share and to look for any unfamiliar words that might create a problem in their reading. Give students approximately 30 seconds to browse the entire story.
- Briefly discuss the information students gathered while browsing. If necessary, go through the story page-by-page while discussing what students see in the pictures and adding any additional "problem" words to word cards. Some problem words may include *piece, watermelon, chocolate, creamed,* and *demanded*.
- Review the word cards with students.

First Reading

- Read the title, author's name, and illustrator's name to students. Have students place their finger under the words as you read them.

- Read the title page. Continue reading the rest of the book, stop to model reading strategies by thinking aloud where you feel it is appropriate. Ask students what good readers do to decode unfamiliar words and to help them understand the book. If students are not sure, have them refer to their Reading Strategies Bookmark (page 11).

- Pause after pages 3 and 4 to allow students to take a close look at the picture. Ask students what they notice about both halves of the pizza. Ask if they think the pieces are equal. Model a "thinking aloud" strategy. For example, say *It looks like Dog tricked Cat into thinking Cat is getting more of the pizza because Cat has two pieces. But the pieces look to me like they are equal in size.*
- Encourage students to look at Cat and Dog's facial expressions. Ask students if they think Cat realizes that Dog is eating the same amount as Cat.

Discussion

- Discuss the predictions students made and the actual outcome of the story.
- Discuss students' reactions to the story or connections students made while reading the story.

Second Reading

- Determine the way you would like to conduct the second reading depending on the ability of your group. Choose one of the following:
  - ✓ Have students choral read with you.
  - ✓ Have students read aloud at their own pace.
  - ✓ Have students read with a partner.

Mini–Language Lesson

- Ask students why they think an exclamation point is used.
- Introduce quotation marks. Tell students that the purpose of a quotation mark is to show that a character is speaking.

Follow-up Activity

- Ask students to choose which character they would rather have lunch with and explain why.

Long Ago and Today

SAMPLE LESSON—NONFICTION, EMERGENT LEVEL

Purpose
- Compare and contrast people of today and long ago
- Identify present and past tense predicates
- Identify the three sounds of -*ed*
- Identify elements of nonfiction books

Key Concept
- time—long ago, today

Vocabulary
farmers, plow, fields, live, travel, hunt, cook

Story Introduction and Story/Picture Walk

- Read the title, the author's name, and the illustrator's name.
- Talk about the picture on the cover. Ask *What is meant by long ago and today? What do you think the book will be about? What type of book is this likely to be and why?*
- Ask students what people of long ago were like and how those people were different than people today. Then, ask students how people of long ago are similar to people today. Write students' responses on the chalkboard or chart paper.
- Show the title page. Say *The title of this book is* Long Ago and Today.
- Show pages 2 and 3. Ask *How are farmers of long ago different from today's farmers? How are they the same?*

Long ago, farmers plowed the fields.   Today, farmers plow the fields.

- Show pages 4–9. Ask *How are people of long ago and people of today alike? How are they different?*
- Show pages 10 and 11. Ask *How are families of long ago and families of today alike? How are they different?*
- Show pages 12–16. Ask *How are children of long ago and children of today alike? How are they different?*

First Reading

- Say *Let's read our story to find out how people, families, and children of long ago and today are alike and different.*
- Read the title, the author's name, and the illustrator's name on the cover. Read the title page.

Long ago, people lived in houses.   Today, people live in houses.

- Read pages 2–5. Point to vocabulary and action words that show past and present tense as you read each page.
- Read pages 6–15. Pause to let students say each action word. Ask *How are the action words for long ago and for today different?*

Long ago, children went to school.

Today, children go to school.

- Read page 16. Ask students to look at the picture and complete the sentence frames *Long ago, children* _____. *Today, children* _____.

Second Reading

- Ask students to read the title, the author's name, and the illustrator's name with you.
- Read the title page together.
- Have students read aloud with a partner. Ask one student to read the "long ago" pages and the other student to read the "today" pages. Then, have students switch roles and read the book again.

Discussion

- Compare the list of students' ideas of how people, families, and children of long ago and today are alike and different to what was mentioned in the book. Place a star next to each idea (on the chart or chalkboard) that was the same.
- Add ideas from the book to the chart or chalkboard.

Mini–Language Lesson

- Have students identify and write the action words that indicate past and present tense. Ask what has been added to the present tense words to make them past tense words (i.e., *-ed*). Ask why *-ed* was not added to the word *go.*

Follow-up Activity

- Have students write their own sentences to compare children of long ago and today by completing the sentence frames *Long ago, children* _____. *Today, children* _____. Invite them to illustrate each sentence. Combine students' completed pages to create a class book.

How & Why Animals Hide

SAMPLE LESSON—NONFICTION, FLUENT LEVEL

Purpose
- Use the following reading strategies: visual screening, sounding out, analyzing sentence structure
- Properly use punctuation, capitalization, and paragraphing
- Identify adjectives

Key Concepts
- the way animals protect themselves

Vocabulary
- star-nosed, burrow, fleshy, dangerous, camouflage, moray eel, speckled, katydid, mimicry, viceroy caterpillar, frothy

Story Introduction
- Give each student a copy of the book.
- Read the title, the author's name, and the photographer's name.
- Have students discuss what they already know about why animals hide.
- Give students approximately 15 seconds to look at the cover. Then, ask them to tell you about what they see.
- Ask students what they think the book will be about. Tell them that this is a nonfiction book. Ask students how they can tell that it is a nonfiction book.
- Read the information about the author and photographer on the back cover.

Story/Picture Walk
- Have students browse through the pages for approximately 30 seconds.
- Ask students to discuss the information they gathered from browsing.
- Introduce vocabulary to help students comprehend the science concepts. Write the words on index cards to create word cards.
- Review the word cards with students. Make sure students can read and understand the words so that they can use their fluency and comprehension of the new science concepts during the first reading of the book.

The hermit crab also hides in a shell. Unlike the turtle, it does not have a shell of its own. Instead, it uses a shell left by another ocean animal.

This shell is just the right size for the hermit crab. The crab tucks its body in tightly to hide from danger. When the hermit crab grows, it will need to find a bigger shell.

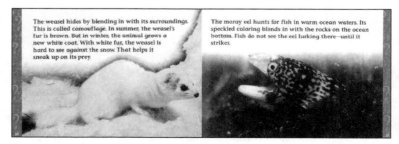

The weasel hides by blending in with its surroundings. This is called camouflage. In summer, the weasel's fur is brown. But in winter, the animal grows a new white coat. With white fur, the weasel is hard to see against the snow. That helps it sneak up on its prey.

The moray eel hunts for fish in warm ocean waters. Its speckled coloring blends in with the rocks on the ocean bottom. Fish do not see the eel lurking there—until it strikes.

First Reading

The star-nosed mole hides underground. It digs a burrow with its strong claws and uses its strange, fleshy nose to feel its way around.

A flying squirrel hides in a hole in a tree. It spends the day there and comes out at night to look for food.

The world can be a dangerous place for little animals such as the squirrel and mole. Bigger animals might want to eat them. Their hiding places keep them safe.

- Read the title, the author's name, and the photographer's name. Have students place their finger under the words as you read them.
- Have students locate the title page and read it with you.
- Continue reading the rest of the book. Stop to model reading strategies by thinking aloud. For example, on page 2, say *I've never seen a star-nosed mole. I think I'll use the picture to help me visualize what one looks like. I can't imagine using my nose to feel my way around.*
- Use students' prior knowledge to help students with their reading comprehension throughout the book.
- Point out the use of context clues. Apposition is when the author defines a word within the sentence or the following sentence. For example, read from page 10 the sentences *The weasel hides by blending in with its surroundings. This is called camouflage.*
- Ask students to practice using context clues to help them figure out what the meaning of *mimicry* is.

Discussion

- Discuss any new science concepts that students learned.
- Discuss students' reactions to the story or connections that students made while reading.
- Answer the "how & why" questions on page 16 of the book.

Second Reading

- Determine the way you would like to conduct the second reading depending on the ability of your group. Choose one of the following:
  - ✓ Have students choral read with you.
  - ✓ Have students read aloud at their own pace.
  - ✓ Have students read with a partner.
- Praise and prompt students' use of reading strategies and their use of thinking aloud.

Mini–Language Lesson

- Ask students to define an adjective. Conduct an adjective word hunt. Some adjectives in this story are *little, bigger, hard, hungry, frothy, brown, new, white, warm, speckled, gray,* and *plain.*

Guided Reading Lesson Plan Template

Book Title_____ Level _____

Purpose _____

_____

Key Concept(s) _____

Vocabulary _____

Story Introduction

_____

_____

_____

_____

_____

_____

Story/Picture Walk

_____

_____

_____

_____

_____

_____

First Reading

_____

_____

Questions to Ask_____

_____

_____

Second Reading

_____

_____

Discussion Topics _____

_____

_____

Mini–Language Lesson

_____

_____

_____

Follow-up Activities

_____

_____

_____

_____

Discussion and Questions

Introduce and discuss the story with students to provide support and background knowledge for students to rely on when they read the text. Ask open-ended questions that will stimulate discussion and build anticipation of the story line or idea. The following are suggested questions and discussion topics. You do not need to ask or discuss each one before a guided reading session. Think carefully about the ability of the group you are working with, and ask questions accordingly.

- Set the scene. Introduce the main topic of the story by showing real objects. For example, before reading a book about basketball, show students an actual basketball, and pass it around to provoke a discussion about students' experiences with basketball.
- Have students discuss what they already know about a topic and/or their prior experiences.
- Have them discuss a recent event, a topic of interest, the title of the text, the illustrations, the author, the main characters, or place names.
- Discuss unfamiliar words and concepts.
- Discuss particular reading strategies you want students to focus on.
- Have students do a picture walk and make predictions about the story.
- Read the title and the names of the author and illustrator. Briefly discuss each.
- Tell students the purpose or goal for reading a particular book.

Types of Questions to Ask

- What do you see on the cover?
- Do you see any familiar words in the title?
- Do you see any words that are a problem for you?
- Is there anything in the pictures that you are wondering about or confused about?
- What do you think this book is going to be about?
- What type of book (e.g., fiction, nonfiction, fantasy) is it likely to be?

Activities

Vocabulary Hunt Give each student a pipe cleaner and a piece of curling ribbon. Have students make a "word wand" by making a loop in one end of their pipe cleaner and tying curling ribbon around the loop. Ask students to use their word wand to point to any unfamiliar words in the book. Write those words on the chalkboard. Then, discuss some of those words with students before they read the book.

Materials
- ✔ pipe cleaners
- ✔ curling ribbon

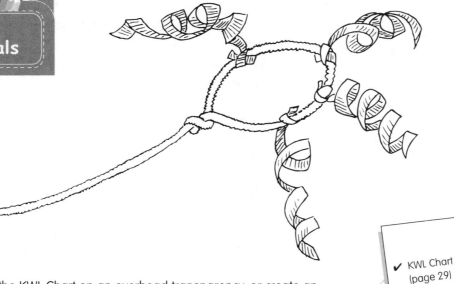

KWL Copy the KWL Chart on an overhead transparency, or create an enlarged version of the reproducible on the chalkboard or a piece of chart paper. Show students the cover of the book, and ask them what they know about the book just by looking at the cover. Write their responses in the first column of the chart. Then, ask students what they want to know about the story and what they think will happen. Write those responses in the second column of the chart. Save the chart, and fill in the last column after students have finished reading the book.

Materials
- ✔ KWL Chart (page 29)
- ✔ overhead transparency or chart paper

What We Already **K**now	What We **W**ant to Know	What We **L**earned
Animals hide to protect themselves	Where do animals hide?	Camoufl… is when animals … in with … surrou…

Activities

Materials

- paper crumpled into balls
- small pieces of cloth
- tape
- toilet-paper tubes
- yarn

Tell a Picture

Make a "microphone" for every two students by wrapping a paper ball in cloth and taping the ends closed. Stuff the cloth into one end of a toilet-paper tube. Use a piece of tape to attach a piece of yarn to the other end of the tube. Explain that one way to make reading easier is to observe all the pictures and learn about the story before reading. Model how to "tell a picture." Point to the cover of a book, and hold up a microphone. Speak into the microphone, and make a prediction about the story's plot based on the cover illustration. Divide the group into pairs, and give each pair a book and a microphone. Have one student in each pair use the microphone and make a prediction about the first page of the book. Ask partners to take turns making predictions. Continue the activity until students have made predictions about the entire book.

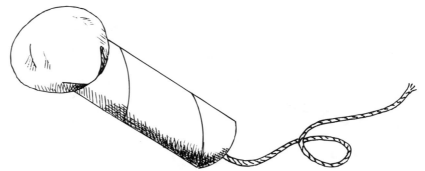

Prior Knowledge

Discuss the cover of a nonfiction book. Walk students through the book, discussing each picture. Invite students to think about the topic and brainstorm words that might appear in the book. Record the words on a piece of chart paper, and read the list aloud. Explain that one way to avoid reading mistakes is to read the title and look at the pictures before you read and predict words that might appear in the story. As students read the text, place a dot sticker on the chart next to each word that appears in the book. This will show students how many words they predicted correctly.

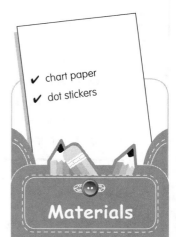

Materials

- chart paper
- dot stickers

Farmer ●
chicken ●
cow ●
dog
rooster ●
barn ●
horse
fence

Barnyard Math with Farmer Fred

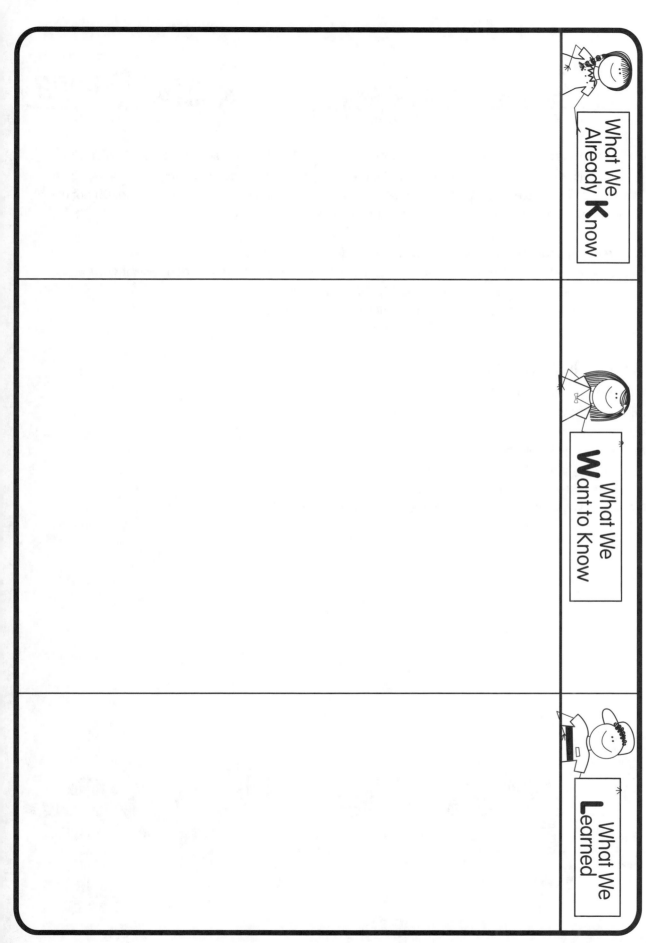

KWL Chart

What We Already **K**now

What We **W**ant to Know

What We **L**earned

During

Discussion and Questions

As students read the text, evaluate and support their use of various reading strategies. Provide students with necessary feedback, or prompt them to use a specific reading strategy. The following are suggested questions and discussion topics to help guide students through their reading. Do not ask every student every question. Evaluate each student, and ask questions accordingly.

- Model reading strategies by "thinking aloud" (see example on page 19).
- Discuss strategies that will help students to decode words. For example, ask students *What word would make sense? Does that look right? What sound do you hear at the beginning of that word?*
- Have students point to the title. Ask them to point to the words and read.

Types of Questions to Ask
- Where do you start reading?
- Which way do you go?
- Can you point to _____?
- What do you think will happen next?
- What do you already know that might help?
- Do you know a word like that?
- What letter would you expect to see at the beginning? At the end?

Materials

- ✔ construction paper bookmarks
- ✔ scissors

Word Frames

In advance, cut a rectangular hole in the center of a construction paper bookmark for each student. As students read, have them frame certain words with their word-frame bookmark. This activity helps students break a big word into smaller parts. For example, have students frame only the root word and then slide the frame over to also show the suffix.

Spiders, spiders every here.

Eye Spy

Have each student glue a wiggly eye to a craft stick. Have students use their craft stick as a bookmark while they follow along during guided reading. Ask them to locate a given word or sound out a word with their "Eye Spy" stick.

Materials

- ✔ wiggly eyes
- ✔ glue
- ✔ craft sticks

Materials

- ✔ none

Thumbs Up!

Write a sight word or letter sound on the chalkboard. While students follow along during guided reading, have them put their thumb up in the air when they hear the sight word or letter sound. This activity will help students stay focused during the reading.

Discussion and Questions

After students read the text, evaluate their comprehension of a story. Ask them questions, or have them participate in activities that ask them to reflect about the story. The following are suggested comprehension activities and questions to check for students' understanding of the story.

- Have students refer to the KWL chart that they completed before guided reading (see page 27). Ask them to discuss what they learned. Write their responses in the third column, "What We Learned," to complete the chart.
- Ask students to compare the predictions that they made before reading the story to what actually happened in the story.
- Invite students to write a summary of the story in their journals.

Types of Questions to Ask

- Who was the main character?
- Describe the main character.
- What is the setting of the story?
- Tell about three events that happened in the story.
- What was your favorite part of the story?
- Have you ever read another story that is similar to this story? How were the stories the same? How were the stories different?
- Was there conflict in the story? If so, what was the problem? How was the conflict solved?
- What else could have happened?
- Is the story fiction or nonfiction?
- How did the story end?
- Why do you think the author ended the story that way?
- Think of a new way to end the story.
- Tell about a similar incident that has happened to you.
- Who was your favorite character and why?
- Why do you think the author decided to include a specific character in the story?

Activities

✔ Prove It reproducible (page 36)

✔ chart paper (optional)

Materials

Prove It

After reading a story, have students discuss the characters. Brainstorm with the class words that describe each character (e.g., words that tell how each character looks, feels, or acts). Record student responses on the chalkboard or a piece of chart paper. Give each student a Prove It reproducible. Ask students to select an important character from the story and write the character's name or draw the character's picture on the reproducible. Ask students to choose two character traits written on the chalkboard or chart paper and then reread the book to find examples that illustrate the traits they selected. Have them write about or draw the parts of the story that illustrate the two traits. Invite students to discuss their character analysis with a partner.

Character Collage

Ask each student to select a character from a book that he or she has recently read. Give each student a piece of construction paper and a magazine. Have students write the name of their character in the center of the construction paper. Then, have them look through their magazine to find pictures and words that they think represent their character. Invite students to cut out these images and words and glue them on their paper around the name of their character. Have students fill the page with images to create a collage. Give each student an opportunity to share his or her collage with the class.

✔ construction paper

✔ magazines

✔ scissors

✔ glue

Materials

✔ index cards

Materials

Cue Cards (Retelling)

Write each of the following words on a separate index card: *Who? When? Where? What? Why?* and *How?* Laminate the cards for durability. Demonstrate a retelling of a story that students read during guided reading by using the cue cards as a guide. Present the cards in the following order: Who? When? Where? What? Why? and How? Use the words to teach students how to discuss first the main characters and setting, then the main theme of the story, and finally the higher-level issues of how and why. Discuss with students how the cards were helpful in remembering the events of the story.

Who? When? Where? What? Why? How?

Sequencing

Write the sentences from a leveled book on sentence strips. Cut apart each sentence, and give the sentence strips to a small group of students. Explain that stories are written in a specific order so they make sense to the reader. Invite students to put the sentences in sequential order. After they have sorted the sentences, have them read the actual leveled book to check their work.

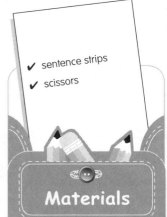

✔ sentence strips
✔ scissors

Materials

On Monday morning, Dog made cookies.

On Monday afternoon, Cat ate the cookies.

On Tuesday morning, Dog made sandwiches.

After

✔ Story Map Cards (page 37)

✔ scissors

Materials

In-the-Book Story Map

Give each student a set of Story Map Cards. Have students cut apart the cards. After students have read and discussed a book, have them reread the book and place the appropriate story map card on the page where that story element appears. Discuss the story elements, and show where they take place in the story. Invite students to rearrange any cards they misplaced.

✔ "Sense-ing" the Story Setting reproducible (page 38)

✔ crayons or markers

Materials

"Sense-ing" the Setting

After reading a story, discuss the setting. Encourage students to picture the setting in their mind. Ask them to picture what the setting would look like, how it would smell, what sounds they might hear, and what they might touch and eat if they were really there. Have students share what they pictured. Give each student a "Sense-ing" the Story Setting reproducible. Have students follow the directions to draw the story setting and write about it.

looks beautiful

smells salty

feels wet and grainy

Name _____ Date _____

Prove It

Choose an important character to draw or write about.

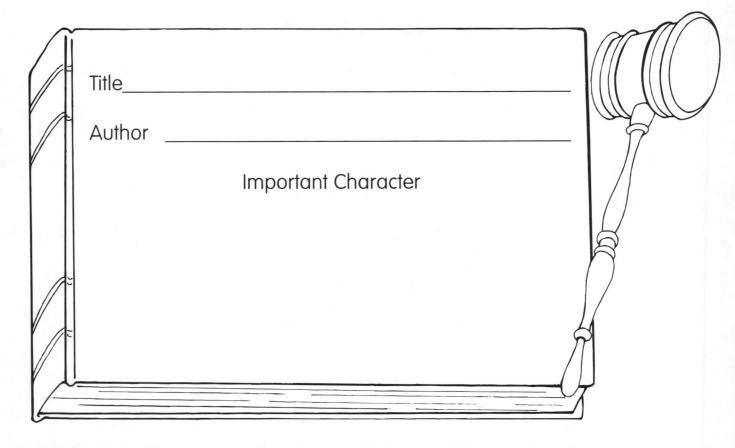

Title _____

Author _____

Important Character

List words that describe the character.	List examples from the story.
1. _____	
2. _____	

Story Map Cards

Introduction
(Characters and Setting)

Main Event One

Main Event Two

Problem

Solution

Ending

Name _____ Date _____

"Sense-ing" the Story Setting

Where does your story take place (setting)? Draw a picture of the story setting in the box. List what you would see, hear, smell, taste, feel, and know about if you could go there.

The story setting: _____

👁 I see _____.

👂 I hear _____.

👃 I smell _____.

👅 I taste _____.

✋ I feel _____.

🧠 I know _____.

Writing Activities

Have students practice their writing skills by completing these fun writing activities. Use the activities in conjunction with your guided reading sessions.

Activities

Materials
- ✔ chart paper (optional)
- ✔ paper
- ✔ crayons or markers

Writing Frames
After reading a book with a reading group, have students use writing frames to create their own text innovations. Write a sentence frame (e.g., *I can read* _____.) on the chalkboard or a piece of chart paper. Ask students to brainstorm a list of possible words (e.g., *a book, magazines, the sign*) to fill in the blank. Write those words below the sentence frame. Give each student a sheet of paper, and ask students to write their own text innovations using the sentence frame and brainstorm list. Invite them to illustrate their sentences.

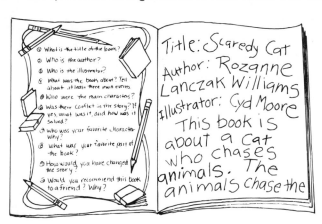

Literary Journal
Make a copy of the Literary Journal Questions reproducible for every two students, and cut apart the question sheets. Give each student a journal and a question sheet. Have students glue their sheet on the inside front cover of their journal. After students read a book, have them use the questions as a guideline to write about that book.

Materials
- ✔ Literary Journal Questions reproducible (page 41)
- ✔ scissors
- ✔ student journals
- ✔ glue

✔ paper
✔ construction paper (optional)

Materials

Prediction Journal
Staple several sheets of paper together, or bind paper in a construction paper cover to make a journal for each student. Before guided reading, have students write what they think the story will be about on the left-hand side of their journal. Then, after students read the book, have them write what the story was about on the right-hand side of their journal.

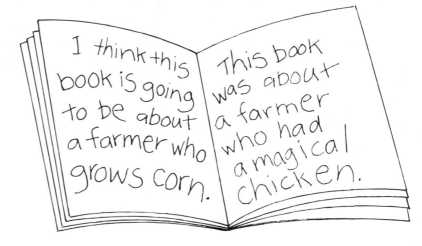

I think this book is going to be about a farmer who grows corn.

This book was about a farmer who had a magical chicken.

Book Character Prescription
Give each student a Prescription Pad reproducible. Have students fill out a "prescription" for a book character. Remind students that the prescriptions should be based on information they know about the character. For example, after a student reads *The Tale of Peter Rabbit* by Beatrix Potter, he or she may prescribe dry clothes, bed rest, and tea for Peter Rabbit. Or, have students create a recipe that reflects the tastes and personality of a book character. For example, a student may create a recipe for garden soup for Peter Rabbit. Ask students to write their recipe on a large index card. Place the completed cards in a recipe box, and invite other students to read them.

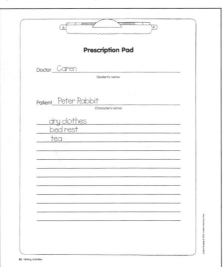

Prescription Pad

Doctor _Caren_
(Student's name)

Patient _Peter Rabbit_
(Character's name)

dry clothes
bed rest
tea

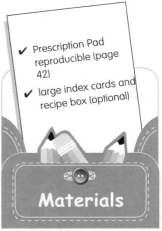

✔ Prescription Pad reproducible (page 42)
✔ large index cards and recipe box (optional)

Materials

Literary Journal Questions

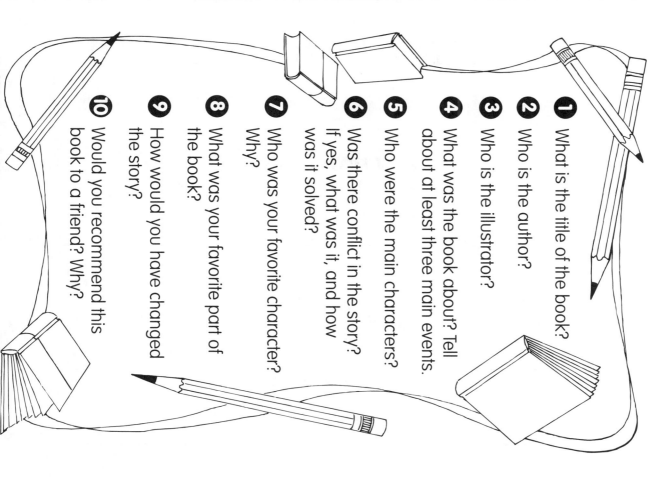

1. What is the title of the book?

2. Who is the author?

3. Who is the illustrator?

4. What was the book about? Tell about at least three main events.

5. Who were the main characters?

6. Was there conflict in the story? If yes, what was it, and how was it solved?

7. Who was your favorite character? Why?

8. What was your favorite part of the book?

9. How would you have changed the story?

10. Would you recommend this book to a friend? Why?

---

1. What is the title of the book?

2. Who is the author?

3. Who is the illustrator?

4. What was the book about? Tell about at least three main events.

5. Who were the main characters?

6. Was there conflict in the story? If yes, what was it, and how was it solved?

7. Who was your favorite character? Why?

8. What was your favorite part of the book?

9. How would you have changed the story?

10. Would you recommend this book to a friend? Why?

Prescription Pad

Doctor _____

(Student's name)

Patient_____

(Character's name)

_____

_____

_____

_____

_____

_____

_____

_____

_____

_____

_____

_____

Using Leveled Books for Other Reading Formats

Not only are leveled books perfect for guided reading, but you can use them for other reading formats as well. Use the books for independent, shared, and home reading activities.

Independent Reading

Book Boxes Encourage independent reading by storing books in color-coded book boxes. Arrange the books by readability level. Assign each reading group a color-coded box. After a group has finished reading a book in a guided reading session, place a copy of that book in the group's book box. Invite students to reread the books from their box during independent reading time.

Chairs Pairs Reading

After students have read a book in guided reading groups, have each student reread the book with a partner. Ask each pair of students to place their chair backs in opposite directions (as shown). Give each pair a copy of the book. While one student reads a page, have the other student follow along. Have partners switch roles for each page until they finish the book. If there is a significant amount of text on a page, have partners alternate reading after every paragraph or after every two or three sentences.

Shared Reading

Materials
- ✔ sentence strips
- ✔ large pieces of chart or butcher paper
- ✔ glue
- ✔ crayons or markers
- ✔ bookbinding materials

Making a Big Book

Create a Big Book version of a leveled book with your students. Assign one page of the book to each student. Give each student a sentence strip for each sentence on his or her page. Have students write their sentence(s) on their strip(s). Give each student a piece of chart or butcher paper. Have students glue their strip(s) at the bottom of their page and then illustrate their sentence(s). As a group, sequence the student-made pages, and bind them together to make a class Big Book.

Shared Reading with a Big Book

The first time you read a Big Book to the class, have students listen silently while you track each word with a decorated pointer. Point out the print, and model concepts of print such as left-to-right progression and return sweep. After students hear the text several times, have them join in whenever they are comfortable. Invite a volunteer to use the pointer to lead the group. As students become acquainted with the text, have them read all predictable or familiar text with the support of your voice. Once you complete a story, invite students to discuss what they learned, liked, and disliked and any general thoughts they had.

Materials
- ✔ decorated pointer

Materials

- ✔ Home Reading Log (page 46)
- ✔ resealable plastic bags

Book Bags

Create a "book bag" for each student by writing his or her name on a large resealable plastic bag. Place a copy of the Home Reading Log in each student's bag. Invite students to choose two or three leveled readers to take home each night to read to someone at home. Have students place the books in their bag and take it home. Ask parents to fill in the book titles on the Home Reading Log and sign for each completed book. When students return the books, invite them to take other books home.

Get the Scoop

Invite students to take books home and complete a Get the Scoop reproducible for each book they read. Display the completed forms on a bulletin board near the classroom library, or combine all the completed forms in a binder, and place the binder in the classroom library. Invite students to read their classmates' book reports.

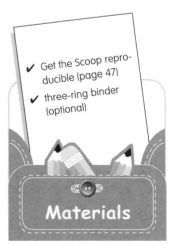

Materials

- ✔ Get the Scoop reproducible (page 47)
- ✔ three-ring binder (optional)

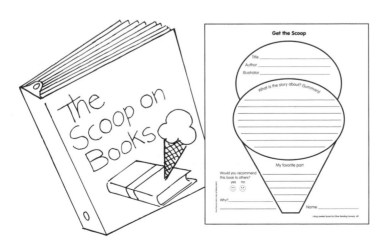

Home Reading Log

Date	Book Title	Number of Pages	Parent Signature

Get the Scoop

Title _____

Author _____

Illustrator _____

What is the story about? (Summary)

_____

_____

_____

_____

_____

_____

_____

_____

My favorite part

_____

Would you recommend
this book to others?

yes   no

Why?_____

_____

Name _____

Assessment

There are several methods of evaluating your students. This section provides an overview of some of the various methods.

Running Records

Running records, developed by Marie Clay as part of the Reading Recovery program, help teachers understand the strategies and cueing systems a reader uses. A running record can also provide information for guided reading instruction, such as how to select text appropriate for instruction and what information to use for grouping students together.

Running records are meant to be done "on the run"—making them possible to do with a classroom full of students.

In a running record, the teacher uses certain conventions to record everything a student says and does while reading a sample text of 100–150 words. For developing readers, complete a running record every 4–6 weeks; for fluent readers, complete a running record every 2–3 months.

Although running records may seem a bit overwhelming at first, they are fairly easy to learn and only require practice on the part of the teacher. A teacher gains evaluative information that is well worth the effort put into learning the process.

After analyzing a running record, a teacher determines the instructional level of the text (whether it is appropriate or too difficult) and what cueing systems the student uses.

Keeping a running record involves close observation of a student while he or she reads selected passages of text and making accurate notes about reading behaviors. This allows you to identify the skills a student uses to make sense of what he or she reads. A running record taken on a familiar text can reveal whether students are reading material at a suitable level of difficulty, if they are making sense of what they read, and how well they use the skills and strategies they have been taught. Using an unfamiliar text can show if a reader takes risks and uses skills independently.

Some teachers prefer to use printed recording sheets, and other teachers simply use blank sheets of paper. A Running Record reproducible (see page 51) is provided for your use. Analyze the record, and calculate the reader's error rate and self-correction rate to determine which previously taught skill the reader is or isn't using to solve meaning-related problems.

Running Record Notations

Use a standard procedure for recording students' reading so that you can compare running records with other teachers. Here are suggested notations to record students' reading in running records.

1 Mark every word read correctly with a check (✓).

2 Record a wrong response by writing the incorrect text above the missed word.

3 If a word is omitted, record it with a dash.

4 If a student tries several times to read a word, record all the tries.

5 If a student repeats a word or phrase, mark it with an "R."

6 If a student corrects a previous error, record it as SC (self-correction).

7 If you need to tell the student a word, mark it with a "T."

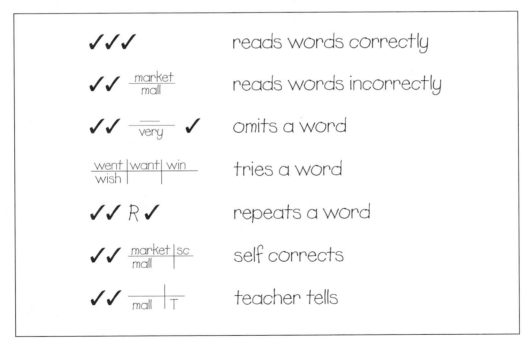

✓ ✓ ✓	reads words correctly
✓ ✓ market/mall	reads words incorrectly
✓ ✓ —/very ✓	omits a word
went | want | win / wish	tries a word
✓ ✓ R ✓	repeats a word
✓ ✓ market | sc / mall	self corrects
✓ ✓ — / mall | T	teacher tells

Scoring and Calculating the Record

Count the running words (RW) in the text. Omit titles. Count the number of errors students made. Incorrectly read words, insertions, omissions, and teacher-told responses count as an error. Repetitions are not scored as an error. Corrected responses count as self-corrections. Subtract the number of errors from the number of running words, divide by the number of running words, and multiply it by 100 to determine the accuracy rate.

$$\text{Accuracy rate} = \frac{RW - E}{RW} \times 100$$

Example: Running words = 150
        Errors = 15

150 − 15 = 135
135/150 = 0.9
0.9 x 100 = 90
The accuracy rate is 90%

The self-correction rate can be determined by counting the total number of self-corrections on the running record. Add that number to the number of errors, and divide by the number of self-corrections to calculate a ratio. For example, if a student makes ten errors and five self-corrections, his or her self-correction ratio would be 1:3.

When a student makes an error or self-correction, note the type of error in the "Analysis of errors and self-corrections" section of the running record. M = meaning, S = structure or syntax, and V = visual. Write *M S V* in the appropriate column. Then, circle the letter that represents the type of error that the student made.

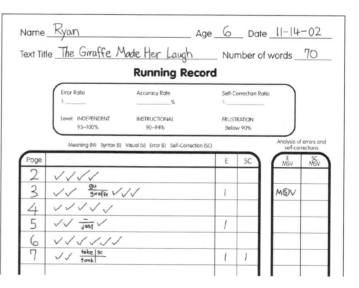

Name _____ Age _____ Date _____

Text Title _____ Number of words _____

Running Record

Error Ratio ($\frac{RW}{E}$)

1: _____

Accuracy Rate ($\frac{RW-E}{RW} \times 100$)

_____%

Self-Correction Ratio ($\frac{E+SC}{SC}$)

1: _____

Level: INDEPENDENT
        95–100%

INSTRUCTIONAL
90–94%

FRUSTRATION
Below 90%

Meaning (M)   Syntax (S)   Visual (V)   Error (E)   Self-Correction (SC)

Analysis of errors and self-corrections

Page		E	SC	E MSV	SC MSV

Other Assessment Methods

The following are other ways that you can assess students' reading skills and behaviors.

Anecdotal Records

Observing students' reading behaviors and writing your observations allows you to identify students' reading patterns and make judgments about their needs. Make several copies of the Anecdotal Records reproducible (page 53), and place them on a clipboard. Carry the clipboard as you observe students, and write down your observations. Then, cut apart the records, and place each student's record in his or her portfolio.

Retelling

Retelling is a strategy to accompany running records and help in the evaluation of a student's comprehension. Instead of questioning students about what they just read, ask them to retell the story orally or in writing as if they were telling the story to someone who has never heard the story before. If a student retells orally, you can evaluate the student's text comprehension, sequencing of ideas, and ability to reconstruct text. If a student retells in writing, then you can also evaluate spelling and grammar.

Reading Inventories

A reading inventory shows a student's progress on a developmental continuum. A teacher observes and records developmental markers, which show patterns of growth. See pages 54–56 for three versions of reading inventories: emergent, early, and fluent.

Checklists

You can create a checklist to assess various classroom behaviors, everything from students' social behaviors to their reading behaviors. A checklist can also help you assess specific skills or tasks. See page 57 for a Concepts about Print checklist. This checklist can be used to assess your entire class. Write each student's name on a line. Mark a check in the appropriate column when a student has learned the skill.

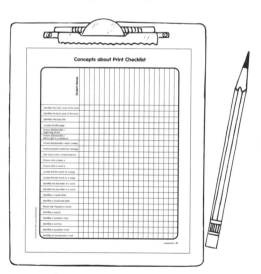

Anecdotal Records

Name _____ Date _____

Name _____ Date _____

Name _____ Date _____

Name _____ Date _____

Emergent Reader Inventory

Name _____

Date of Birth _____

Key
N—Not observed
W—Working toward skill
A—Achieved skill

Emergent Reader Behaviors	Date				Anecdotal Notes
Uses reading-like behavior to approximate book language					
Notices/reads environmental print					
Recognizes some high-frequency words					
Retells favorite stories					
Memorizes rhymes and poems					
Knows what a letter is					
Knows what a word is					
Knows some letters and sounds					
Knows that letter symbols form words					
Knows that text goes left to right					
Knows where to start reading the text					
Is establishing one-to-one correspondence					
Enjoys shared experiences with books					
Enjoys writing					

Early Reader Inventory

| Name _____ |
| Date of Birth _____ |

Early Reader Behaviors	Date				Anecdotal Notes
Has established one-to-one correspondence					
Chooses to read independently					
Expects to get meaning from print					
Takes risks with unfamiliar text					
Reads word-by-word with finger or voice					
Begins to integrate strategies and cross-check cueing systems:					
• Rereads when it doesn't make sense					
• Self-corrects errors					
• Relies on visual cues more than pictures					
Recognizes high-frequency words out of context					
Spells some high-frequency words correctly					
Enjoys writing					
Uses resources to help spell words					
Enjoys shared reading experiences					

Fluent Reader Inventory

Name _____

Date of Birth _____

Fluent Reader Behaviors	Date				Anecdotal Notes
Integrates strategies automatically and cross-checks cueing systems					
Uses strategies flexibly for familiar and unfamiliar text					
Has a large sight word vocabulary					
Moves from reading aloud to reading silently					
Chooses appropriate books for own purposes					
Reads a series of books written by a favorite author					
Reads short chapter books with the support of pictures					
Reads chapter books for longer period of time					
Responses show reflection from different points of view					
Reads books to pursue particular interests					
Reads informational books but still needs support with expository text					
Realizes that different texts demand different strategies					
Is capable of reading different kinds of text across the curriculum					
Reads a variety of sources to independently research a topic					
Has developed an appreciation for fiction and/or nonfiction books					

Concepts about Print Checklist

	Student Names																			
Identifies the front cover of the book																				
Identifies the back cover of the book																				
Identifies the book title																				
Locates the title page																				
Knows directionality—beginning of text																				
Knows directionality—left-to-right in a sentence																				
Knows directionality—return sweep																				
Knows that print carries the message																				
Has one-to-one correspondence																				
Knows what a letter is																				
Knows what a word is																				
Locates the first word on a page																				
Locates the last word on a page																				
Identifies the first letter of a word																				
Identifies the last letter of a word																				
Identifies a capital letter																				
Identifies a lowercase letter																				
Reads high-frequency words																				
Identifies a period																				
Identifies a question mark																				
Identifies a comma																				
Identifies a quotation mark																				
Identifies an exclamation mark																				

Fiction Leveled Books

Book Level	Grade Level	Book Title	Subject Matter
B	K–1	Pigs	counting, rhyming
B	K–1	Under the Sky	plants
C	K–1	All Through the Week with Cat and Dog	days of the week, food
C	K–1	Barney Bear Gets Dressed	color words, clothing items
C	K–1	Cat and Dog	friendship, painting
C	K–1	The Giraffe Made Her Laugh	rhyming
C	K–1	How Many?	counting
C	K–1	Mr. Noisy Builds a House	shelter
C	K–1	On the Go	transportation
C	K–1	Pug's Hugs	phonics—v, y, short u
C	K–1	Scaredy Cat	feelings
C	K–1	What Comes in Threes?	number sense, counting
C	K–1	Where Do Monsters Live?	colors, adjectives
C	K–1	Where's Your Tooth?	losing teeth, quotation marks
C	K–1	Whose Forest Is It?	habitat preservation
D	1	Bears, Bears, Everywhere	bears, rhyming
D	1	Cinderella Dressed in Yellow	colors, numbers, rhyming
D	1	City Mouse and Country Mouse	comparing
D	1	The Colors of My Day	colors, daily schedule
D	1	Five Little Monsters	counting, number concepts
D	1	A Great Attitude	moods, emotions
D	1	Hap and Cap	phonics—p, n, short a
D	1	I Can't Sleep	matter
D	1	I Spy	phonics—m, f, s, r, h, t, c, short a
D	1	Jet It, Get It	phonics—z, x, short e
D	1	Little Green Frog	quotation marks
D	1	Mom Can Fix Anything	tools
D	1	Mr. Noisy	noises, cooperation
D	1	Pom-Pom's Big Win	phonics—w, k, short i
D	1	Rain	rain
D	1	Safety Counts!	safety, counting
D	1	Scaredy Cat Runs Away	sequencing, measuring
D	1	Spiders, Spiders Everywhere!	counting, one-to-one correspondence
D	1	Twice as Nice	phonics
D	1	Way Down South	rhyming, bugs
D	1	What's Going On?	five senses
D	1	What's In My Pocket?	matter, texture, shape, size
D	1	Where Are You Going?	five senses

D	1	Who Will Help?	teamwork, cooperation
D	1	Who's Hiding?	animal survival
E	1	Barney Bear, World Traveler	transportation, geography
E	1	The Bear Went Over the Mountain	repetition, positional words
E	1	Can You Read a Map?	maps
E	1	Cat and Dog at School	school, social skills
E	1	Cat and Dog: The Super Snack	food, cooperation
E	1	Click, Click	phonics—qu, ck
E	1	Down on the Farm	animal sounds
E	1	Five Little Monsters Went to School	school, social skills
E	1	I Need to Clean My Room	hygiene, chores
E	1	If a Tree Could Talk	protecting the environment
E	1	The Little Green Man Visits a Farm	farm, animal sounds
E	1	The Little Green Man Visits Pine Cone Cove	phonics—long o: o-e, oa, ow; -old
E	1	The Monsters' Tea Party	repetition, imagination
E	1	Mr. Noisy's Book of Patterns	patterns, onomatopoeia
E	1	Mr. Noisy's Helpers	jobs, responsibility
E	1	Pete's Street Beat	phonics—long e: ee, e-e, ea, ending e
E	1	Sing-Song Sid	phonics— -ing, -ong, -ang
E	1	Top Job, Mom!	phonics—b, d, g, l, j, short o
F	1	A-Counting We Will Go	counting, number concepts
F	1	Apron Annie in the Garden	science—living and nonliving things
F	1	Barney Bear's Party	phonics—r-controlled vowels
F	1	By Myself or with My Friends	cooperation, teamwork
F	1	The Costume Parade	ordinal numbers
F	1	Dave and Jane's Band	phonics—long a: ay, a-e, ai
F	1	Detective Dog and the Search for Cat	maps
F	1	Dinosaurs Dancing	numbers, rhyming
F	1	Draw and Share	phonics—consonant digraphs: sh, ch, th
F	1	Good Choices for Cat and Dog	needs and wants
F	1	I Have a New Baby Brother	animal babies
F	1	I Love the Mountains	environment
F	1	If We Could Do What the Animals Do	animals—habitats, adaptations
F	1	Just Like Me	cultural diversity
F	1	Matthew the Magician	magnets
F	1	Mr. Noisy Paints His House	colors
F	1	Out to Gumball Pond	phonics—ew; ou as in *out*; ow as in *now*
F	1	Pack a Picnic	weather, colors
F	1	Sad Sam and Blue Sue	phonics—oo, ue
F	1	She'll Be Coming Around the Mountain	repetition
F	1	There's a Monster in the Tree	repetition, rhyme
F	1	This Is the Way	good health and hygiene
F	1	What Do We Need?	social studies
F	1	What Do You See?	numbers, body parts
F	1	What Happened?	solid, liquid, gas

F	1	Who Took the Cookies from the Cookie Jar?	counting by twos, subtraction
G	1	The ABC Bags	phonics—double f, l, and s
G	1	Be a Friend	character education—friendship
G	1	Cat and Dog at the Circus	phonics—question words, soft c and g
G	1	Cat and Dog Go Shopping	size comparisons
G	1	Following the Rules	character education—respect
G	1	The Hungry Farmer	quotation marks
G	1	I Paint Blue	colors
G	1	If Animals Came to School	school, animals
G	1	Jo Jo in Outer Space	phonics—simple word endings: -er, -ed, -ly, -y
G	1	Mr. Noisy at the Dude Ranch	phonics—long u: u-e; /oi/ sound: oi, oy
G	1	The Rainy Day Band	phonics—contractions
G	1	Rickety Rock around the Clock	time
G	1	Riddle and Rhyme with Apron Annie	phonics—rhyming words, two-syllable words
G	1	Splish, Splash	phonics—three-letter blends: str, spl, and scr
G	1	Think Before You Act	character education—self-control
H	1–2	Apron Annie's Pies	subtraction
H	1–2	Cat and Dog Make the Best, Biggest, Most Wonderful Cheese Sandwich	food, superlatives
H	1–2	Counting Kittens	counting
H	1–2	Dare to Have Courage	character education—courage
H	1–2	The Farmer Didn't Wake Up	animal sounds, repetition
H	1–2	Lemonade	liquid measurement, frogs
H	1–2	Magical, Miracle Me	self-esteem
H	1–2	Monster Stew	cooperation
H	1–2	Never Give Up	character education—perseverance
H	1–2	Patterns All around Me	patterns
H	1–2	Rhythm, Rhythm	rhythmic beat
H	1–2	Ten Monsters in a Bed	counting, subtraction
H	1–2	The Ten-Second Race	linear measurement
H	1–2	Truck Tricks	phonics—consonant blends: tr, gr, dr, cr, fl
H	1–2	Where Did It Go?	properties of matter
H	1–2	Would It Be Right?	character education—good judgement
H	1–2	You Can Count on Me	character education—responsibility
I	1–2	Barnyard Math with Farmer Fred	math in the "real world"
I	1–2	Baseball Cards and Piggy Banks	money
I	1–2	The Bugs Go Marching	pattern counting, multiplication, sorting
I	1–2	Electric Car	transportation
I	1–2	Everyone Is Special and Unique	character education—acceptance
I	1–2	The Fox and the Chicken	getting along
I	1–2	Grandmother's Garden	cultural diversity
I	1–2	I'm a Can-Do Kid	self-esteem
I	1–2	Show You Understand	character education—compassion
I	1–2	Working Together	character education—cooperation
J	2	Lunch with Cat and Dog	manners, equivalent fractions
J	2	Sharing Is Caring	character education—generosity
J	2	Telling the Truth	character education—honesty

Nonfiction Leveled Books

Book Level	Grade Level	Book Title	Subject Matter
A	K–1	How to Make a Mudpie	following directions
A	K–1	I Can Read	reading
A	K–1	I Can Write	writing
B	K–1	Buttons Buttons	colors, numbers, sorting, size, shape
B	K–1	The Four Seasons	seasons
B	K–1	How's the Weather?	weather
B	K–1	I Am Special	self-esteem
B	K–1	I See Colors	colors
B	K–1	I See Shapes	shapes, patterns
B	K–1	Our Pumpkin	estimating, counting, measurement
B	K–1	See How It Grows	living things, life cycles
B	K–1	We Can Share at School	sharing, school
C	K–1	How Can I Help?	family, responsibility
C	K–1	I See Patterns	patterns, shapes
C	K–1	Is It Alive?	living and nonliving things
C	K–1	Long Ago and Today	times past
C	K–1	We Can Eat the Plants	plant parts
C	K–1	What Do We Need?	people's and animals' needs
C	K–1	Who Lives Here?	animal homes and food
D	1	Families Share	family, cooperation
D	1	It's Melting!	properties and changes in matter
D	1	The One and Only Special Me	self-esteem
D	1	Round and Round the Seasons Go	seasons
D	1	The Seed Song	plant growth
D	1	What Time Is It?	duration of time, number recognition
D	1	What's the Weather Like Today?	weather
D	1	The World in a Supermarket	international trade
E	1	The Block Party	social studies
E	1	Helping Mom and Dad	chores, cooperation
E	1	In Times Long Ago	times past
E	1	It Started as an Egg	life cycles
E	1	Let's Take Care of the Earth	conservation
E	1	My Global Address	geography
E	1	Oranges for Orange Juice	progression of product
E	1	People Say Hello	cultural diversity
E	1	Pilgrim Children Had Many Chores	times past
E	1	Reduce, Reuse, Recycle	recycling, conservation
E	1	Sink or Float?	buoyancy
F	1	100 Years Ago	times past

F	1	Best Friends	friendship, blindness
F	1	Caring for Our Lizard	caring for a pet, animals' needs
F	1	Celebrating Father's Day: Father's Day Is for Special People	holidays, fathers
F	1	Celebrating Mother's Day: Mom's Memory Box	holidays, mothers
F	1	Celebrating Valentine's Day: My Special Valentine	holidays, love
F	1	Collecting Things Is Fun!	attributes
F	1	Did You Know?	times past
F	1	Houses	shelter
F	1	I Try to Be a Good Person	manners, decision making
F	1	It Started As a Seed	plants—life cycles and uses
F	1	Playground Problem Solvers	decision making
G	1	Anthills and Apartments	homes
G	1	Celebrating Chanukah: Eight Nights	Chanukah
G	1	Celebrating Easter: The Easter Egg Hunt	Easter
G	1	Celebrating Thanksgiving: Giving Thanks	Thanksgiving
G	1	I Can Talk with My Hands	sign language
G	1	Look and See	counting, colors, shapes, logic
G	1	Maps	maps, rhyming words
G	1	The Time Song	time, days of the week, seasons
G	1	A Tree is a Home	trees, animals
G	1	We Can Make Graphs	counting, graphing, days of the week
H	1–2	Celebrating Chinese New Year: Nick's New Year	Chinese New Year
H	1–2	Celebrating Christmas: Christmas Decorations	Christmas
H	1–2	Let's Measure It!	linear measurement
H	1–2	Measurement Mysteries	measurement
I	1–2	Celebrating Cinco de Mayo: Fiesta Time!	holidays
I	1–2	Celebrating Patriotic Holidays: Honoring America	holidays
I	1–2	Celebrating Presidents' Day: What Is a President?	holidays
I	1–2	The Crayola® Counting Book	place value; counting by ones, twos, fives, and tens; sorting
I	1–2	Just Graph It!	graphing, comparisons
I	1–2	Little Number Stories: Addition	counting by ones, twos, and tens; addition
I	1–2	Little Number Stories: Subtraction	counting, subtraction
I	1–2	Numbers All around Me	number recognition, environmental print
I	1–2	Our Favorites	graphing
J	2	The Magic Money Box	money values
J	2	The Skip Count Song	counting by twos, fives, and tens
M	2–3	Celebrating Martin Luther King Jr. Day: Dreaming of Change	Martin Luther King Jr.
N	3	Among the Flowers	habitats
N	3	Animal Feet	animals
N	3	At the Farm	habitats
N	3	At the Pond	habitats
N	3	How & Why Animals Hatch from Eggs	animal reproduction
N	3	How & Why Birds Build Nests	science—shelter
N	3	How & Why Birds Use Their Bills	science—birds, finding food
N	3	How & Why Plants Eat Insects	science—plants
N	3	How & Why Seeds Travel	science—seeds

N	3	How & Why Spiders Spin Silk	science—spiders
N	3	In the Garden	habitats
N	3	In the Park	habitats
O	3	Animal Eyes	animals
O	3	Animal Feathers & Fur	animals
O	3	Animal Noses	animals
O	3	Animal Skin & Scales	animals
O	3	Animal Tails	animals
O	3	At the Zoo	habitats
O	3	Bean	life cycles
O	3	Horse	life cycles
O	3	How & Why Animals Grow New Parts	science—regeneration
O	3	How & Why Animals Hide	science—protection, camouflage
O	3	How & Why Animals Prepare for Winter	science—hibernation
O	3	Hummingbird	life cycles
O	3	In a Tree	habitats
O	3	In the Meadow	habitats
O	3	Jumping Spider	life cycles
O	3	Plant Blossoms	plants
O	3	Plant Fruits & Seeds	plants
P	3	Animal Ears	animals
P	3	Animal Mouths	animals
P	3	At The Seashore	habitats
P	3	Green Snake	life cycles
P	3	How & Why Animals Are Poisonous	science—protection
P	3	How & Why Insects Grow and Change	science—insects
P	3	How & Why Insects Visit Flowers	pollination, bees, camouflage
P	3	In the Desert	habitats
P	3	Ladybug	life cycles
P	3	Monarch Butterfly	life cycles
P	3	Plant Leaves	plants
P	3	Underfoot	habitats
P	3	Wood Frog	life cycles
Q	3	Chicken	life cycles
Q	3	Fighting Fish	life cycles
Q	3	In the Forest	habitats
Q	3	Maple Tree	life cycles
Q	3	Plant Stems & Roots	plants
Q	3	Sunflower	life cycles

Notes